HUMPTY
Dumpty

FLIP-SIDE
RhYMES

FROM THE POINT OF VIEW
OF THE KING'S MEN

by Christopher Harbo

illustrated by Danny Chatzikonstantinou

raintree

a Capstone company — publishers for children

D0493338

All the king's horses

and all the king's men

Couldn't glue Humpty

together again.

They tried and they tried

So then they gave up

and ate . . .

. . . SCRAMBLED EGGS!

NOW **FLIP** THE BOOK
TO GET ANOTHER SIDE OF THE RHYME.

other titles in this series:

JACK and J:ll
FLIP-Side Rhymes

Little BO PEEP
FLIP-Side Rhymes

Little *Miss* MUFFET
FLIP-Side Rhymes

NOW FLIP THE BOOK
TO GET ANOTHER SIDE OF THE RHYME.

Raintree is an imprint of Capstone Global Library Limited,
a company incorporated in England and Wales having its
registered office at 64 Banbury Road, Oxford, OX2 7DY –
Registered company number: 6695582

www.raintree.co.uk
myorders@raintree.co.uk

Text © Capstone Global Library Limited 2020
The moral rights of the proprietor have been asserted.

All rights reserved. No part of this publication may
be reproduced in any form or by any means (including
photocopying or storing it in any medium by electronic
means and whether or not transiently or incidentally to
some other use of this publication) without the written
permission of the copyright owner, except in accordance
with the provisions of the Copyright, Designs and Patents
Act 1988 or under the terms of a licence issued by the
Copyright Licensing Agency, Barnard's Inn, 86 Fetter
Lane, London, EC4A 1EN (www.cla.co.uk). Applications
for the copyright owner's written permission should be
addressed to the publisher.

Editor: Gillia Olson
Designer: Ashlee Suker
Art Director: Nathan Gassman
Production Specialist: Laura Manthe

The illustrations in this book were created digitally.
Original illustrations © Capstone Global Library Limited
2020
Originated by Capstone Global Library Ltd
Printed and bound in India

ISBN 978 1 4747 9054 3
24 23 22 21 20
10 9 8 7 6 5 4 3 2 1

British Library Cataloguing in Publication Data
A full catalogue record for this book is available from the
British Library.

HIGH LIFE
HIGHLAND LIBRARIES
38001900418454
BERTRAMS   24/09/2019
£6.99
JF
WITHDRAWN

3800 19 0041845 4
HIGH LIFE HIGHLAND

HUMPTY Dumpty

flip-side Rhymes

From the
point of view of
HUMPTY DUMPTY

by Christopher Harbo

illustrated by Danny Chatzikonstantinou

raintree
a Capstone company — publishers for children

Humpty Dumpty

sat on a wall,

Humpty
Dumpty
had a
great fall.

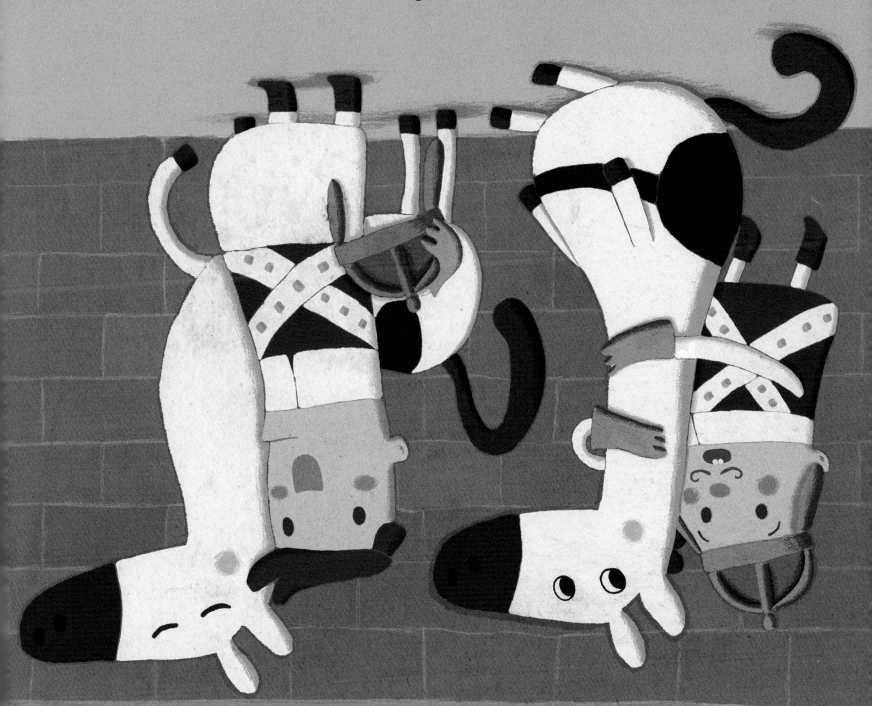

All the king's horses

and all the king's men

couldn't put Humpty together again.